PLATFORM PAPERS

QUARTERLY ESSAYS ON THE PERFORMING ARTS FROM CURRENCY HOUSE

No. 37
November 2013

CURRENCY HOUSE

Platform Papers Partners

We acknowledge with gratitude our Partners in continuing support of Platform Papers and its mission to widen understanding of performing arts practice and encourage change where it is needed:

Gil Appleton
Jane Bridge
Katharine Brisbane
Larry Galbraith
Tony Grierson
Cathy Hunt
Rod MGeogh

To them and to all subscribers and Friends of Currency House we extend our grateful thanks.

Contents

1   NOT AT A CINEMA NEAR YOU:
    Australia's film distribution problem
    LAUREN CARROLL HARRIS

79 Readers' Forum
    Nicole Beyer and Patricia Hoffie on David
    Pledger's *Re-Valuing the Artist in the
    New World Order* (Platform Papers 36)

AVAILABILITY Platform Papers, quarterly essays on the performing arts, is published every February, May, August and November and is available through bookshops, by subscription or online. For details see our website at www.currencyhouse.org.au.

LETTERS Currency House invites readers to submit letters of 400–1,000 words in response to the essays. Letters should be emailed to the Editor at info@currencyhouse.org.au or posted to Currency House at PO Box 2270, Strawberry Hills, NSW 2012, Australia. To be considered for the next issue, the letters must be received by 30 December.

Not at a Cinema Near You

Australia's film distribution problem

||||||||||||||||||||||||||||||||||||||||||||||||||||||||||||||||||||||||||

LAUREN CARROLL HARRIS

About the Author

Lauren Carroll Harris is a writer and artist. Her film and arts reviews have appeared in *RealTime, Screen Hub, Time Out* and online magazines like *Das Platforms*. On Sydney's leading independent radio station, FBi 94.5, she is a regular contributor to *The Picture Show* and formerly wrote and produced documentaries for the award-winning program *All the Best*. The recipient of an Australian Postgraduate Award, Lauren is currently working on a PhD on film distribution at the University of New South Wales, where she completed a Bachelor of Arts (Film Studies; First-Class Honours) and Bachelor of Fine Arts (Painting). Aside from her solo shows at Seventh Gallery, Melbourne, and Kudos Gallery, Sydney, she is a co-director of Archive Space, an artist-run gallery in Sydney.

Acknowledgments

I seriously appreciate the input of my PhD supervisor Greg Dolgopolov, who has shaped my thinking and supported me through hours of emails and very generous conversations. Thank you, Greg. The impact of John Golder's sharp, encouraging and enthusiastic editorial insight has stretched beyond this short publication and taught me a lot about how to think about writing.

I thank the members of the Currency House editorial board, who were prepared to take a risk on a largely untested writer. Advice from Nick Parsons, Nick Shimmin and Katharine Brisbane in the late stages of this researching and drafting process was extremely useful. I also thank Jane Mills for her frank comments and reassurances, and Michelle Langford for her helpful and unprompted research leads. An array of Screen Australia staff has politely endured my streams of questions, emails and phone calls. This paper has also benefited from many interviews and discussions with distributors and film professionals, including Troy Lum, Sophie Raymond, Richard Harris and Simon Cunich. Their experiences and ideas have greatly enriched my thinking.

Introduction

This essay is about how digital and innovative distribution can haul Australian films from the cultural margins into the mainstream. While cinema attendance in general has grown since the 1990s, audiences for Australian films have fallen away. A popular media narrative has dwelt on the apparently dull, depressing and unwatchable nature of most Australian films. I'm going to reframe the discussion. We have conflated the 'film industry' with the 'production sector' and neglected a wholesale analysis of the entire film value chain. Focusing on the question of storytelling has distracted us from the critical arenas of distribution and exhibition—the routes by which films reach their audiences. The Australian film industry is suffering from an archaic approach to film distribution that is maladjusted to the diversifying ways in which audiences access movies. Some filmmakers are offering new solutions to this problem by embracing innovative distribution strategies that are responsive to audiences and focused on easily available means of film delivery. This essay will bring together the lessons of these different experiments and state the case for a new distribution model that can allow local films to expand their audiences and revenues.

The idea that Australian films are boring, greyscale artefacts is not so much a critical analysis as an unhelpful, subjective generalisation. But it has so deeply pervaded the national conversation that it is rarely questioned. Its simplicity belies the complexity of the industry's structure, the myriad stakeholders involved and their conflicting interests and desires. It is also a myth that betrays the diversity of local films produced every year.

This essay will look at something more concrete: where revenue from cinema-ticket stubs flows to. From an $18 ticket, about $11 stays with the exhibitors (a sweet top-up on their popcorn sales), and about $6 goes to the film's distributor (who must sign a film before Screen Australia, the key Federal Government film-funding body, can approve production investment). That leaves $1 to be returned to the filmmakers and private investors, including Screen Australia.[1] In the event of a local film actually recouping its production budget at the box office, the likelihood of Screen Australia, the filmmakers or other stakeholders receiving any return on their investment is vanishingly low. This illustrates how the commercial processes of distribution and exhibition provide some of the structural obstacles that prevent Australian films from reaching any financial self-sustainability. Setting aside the success of a few recent big Australian films, this essay will take a close look at the commercial processes involved.

Why don't theatrical releases seem to work for

local films? The films that do perform well at the box office—lately, *The Sapphires, Red Dog* and *Bran Nue Dae*—have the machinery of hit-making and active distribution behind them. They have wide releases and serious marketing budgets utilised in a thoughtful manner to activate their target audiences. But how many local films have these resources, and what can be done to replace them?

The material constraints of the current theatrical distribution system and methodological problems of how we are disseminating films are rarely scrutinised systematically. Distribution, rather than being an impartial series of mechanisms through which completed films reach their demanding audiences, is in fact a problem requiring innovative solutions for local filmmakers. Distributors do not simply chase demand, they create it, and they do not simply purchase readymade films, they provide upfront investment, have a stake in creative control and influence the kinds of films produced. They are the passage and the roadblock between filmmakers and viewers. Cinema audiences are rarely given the opportunity to choose Australian films, particularly at the dominant exhibition source, the multiplex, as their choices are largely predetermined by distributors and exhibitors who control filmmakers' access to screens. Given the limited availability of cinema screens, it is astonishing that any local film lasts more than a fortnight in theatres. To improve financial sustainability and grow audiences, we need a shift in perspective away from development and production, toward distribution and exhibition. After all, a film is only influential as long as it is available. We need to reframe the discussion of Australian films' shortcomings around the question of increasing their distributive potential, and show how lower-cost, direct-to-viewer distribution models might be constructed.

Against this backdrop is the constant unrolling of digital production, distribution and exhibition techniques. We are currently witnessing an unfolding of media systems, a reorganisation of the old ways of doing and creating. Audiences are splintering between proliferating platforms and devices, DVD sales are dropping away: the traditional systems of film dissemination have been transformed by the digital era, but new ones have yet to be defined. There are, however, a number of films with innovative distribution methods that have managed to reach wide audiences and financial sustainability. These innovatively released films show us what distribution can be and do. They provide signposts for us in rethinking the audience-expanding possibilities for film distribution. Bob Connolly and Sophie Raymond's music documentary *Mrs Carey's Concert* (2011) was issued to cinemas without a distribution company, allowing the filmmakers to craft their own targeted marketing strategy and gain a direct line to ticket sales. The film became the fourth-highest-grossing non-IMAX documentary in Australia's history. Carlos Ledesma's *The Tunnel* (2011) bypassed the box office almost completely, replacing it with informal distribution and financing methods like crowd-funding and file-sharing as *the method* of filmmaking and distribution. Both it and *Mrs Carey's Concert* saw ancillary markets as integral to their audience engagement and release strategies. Cinema is no longer the main site of film-going and has been overtaken by informal, non-theatrical means of distribution: only one in ten films is watched in a cinema.[2]

Whereas previous commentators have asked how we are to get better access to screens, I want to shift the perspective.[3] Based on conversations with distributors and filmmakers, I ask: how can we create our own distribution systems that are accessible to wide audiences and financially sustainable for filmmakers? The possibilities for digital film *production* have been widely discussed by filmmakers wanting inexpensive ways to create, but what about digital film *distribution*?[4] What possibilities exist for the inexpensive, independently controlled, multi-platform delivery of Australian films to reach their distributive potential? Understanding how distribution goes beyond merely transmitting content to audiences, to actually *creating* audiences, is vital to an understanding of how greater demand for local content might be achieved. The myopic focus on production and development has to end: we need a new distribution model for the digital age.

1: Not coming soon to a theatre near you

Historical amnesia: a brief history of Australian distribution

Almost unbelievably, Australia once had one of the world's healthiest national film industries. In the early 1900s we produced more feature films than, and had the largest cinema-going population of, any other country. The rise of a new corporate film production-and-distribution model in the USA in the 1910s had a direct impact on Australia, where imported films were rare. The end of this period was brought on, first, by the exhibition monopoly of Australasian Films known as the 'Combine', which favoured cheap overseas imports over locally funded productions, and second, by the arrival in 1918 of Hollywood distribution arms, which forced cinemas to book entire slates of Hollywood films and squeezed the ability of Australian producers to book screen time. By 1923, 94 per cent of the films screened in Australia were American in origin, a statistic that remains largely unchanged today.[5] Although American ownership of cinemas was not formal, Hollywood's influence in the distribution landscape became entrenched. This enabled a high level of control over mainstream film culture: the era of independent cinemas and abundantly screened local content was fleeting, and the patterns and structures that emerged in the 1910s and 1920s remain in place today.

Since 1918, a number of fruitless attempts have been made to mitigate the cultural impacts of these formative industrial shifts. A procession of Royal Commissions, Tariff Board inquiries and state government hearings has followed an almost identical narrative: independent exhibitors complain about the larger distributors' business practices, recommendations are made, but very few are implemented. Efforts at regulation have been repeatedly defeated by hardcore lobbying from the major distributors. In 1996, the Australian Competition and Consumer Commission (ACCC) conducted an inquiry into the cinema industry, and found Australia's distribution sector more concentrated in ownership than that of the US, Japan and most European countries.[6]

During the 1927 Royal Commission, '[a]llegations from producers, that the 'Combine' did not give Australian producers a fair go, met the usual defence from Australasian Pictures that they could not be expected to release films that were poor quality'.[7] It is a particularly attractive argument to distributors, as it diverts attention from the structural issues, thus benefiting Hollywood product and preventing wider access to Australian content. This highly subjective argument has been actively bolstered over the last hundred years by the major distributors and flows from their basic self-interest to continue disseminating the films of their overseas parent companies.

Fast-forward to 2013. Australian filmmakers remain prisoners of this history. Bottlenecks in the distribution sector are rendering Australian films inaccessible to wide audiences, and there are three major areas creating this problem that remain unaddressed by state and film policymakers.

The first is the stranglehold of the six major distributors—an oligopoly comprised of subsidiaries of the major Hollywood studios. Ninety per cent of films viewed at Australian cinemas are distributed by these companies (see Figure 1). It is almost impossible for local filmmakers to make their films available at multiplexes, as these cinemas have pre-booked slates of product fed to them by their parent and partnered companies. That leaves 30 other companies to distribute the remaining ten per cent of films, including Madman, Dendy, Palace and Hopscotch eOne. Independent and art-house cinemas become the main outlets for local film, but these are feeling the squeeze of the larger distributors' business strategies: '[V]ertical integration and the development of massive economies of scale in both production and distribution [...] provide high barriers to entry for outsiders.'[8] Indeed, independent cinemas decreased in number from 98 in 2001 to 86 in 2013.[9] In an effort to remain competitive, art-houses are now playing more blockbusters like the inescapable teen vampire *Twilight* sagas, and fewer screens are available for Australian or smaller films.

The second major big-picture issue is the scaling-up of the entire global film production-and-distribution apparatus. The trend is toward saturation releases (more than 200 prints across cinemas) for mega-budget

Distributor	2012		
	Box Office	**Market Share**	**No.titles**
Roadshow/Warner Bros	$277.6m	25%	57
Fox	$181.7m	16%	27
Universal	$176.4m	16%	22
Sony	$156.5m	14%	34
Walt Disney	$105.5m	9%	17
Paramount	$97.4m	9%	25
Other	$131.5m	12%	368
Total	**$1,126.7m**	**100%**	**550**

Figure 1. Distributors' market share, 2012

It is clear from the most recently available figures that the monopolisation, patterns and structures that emerged in the distribution sector in the 1910s and 20s remain in place today: the films that reach the widest audiences are those distributed by the major studios' subsidiaries. (Source: Screen Australia)

movies, which *must* perform well in their first week at the cinema or risk being bumped by the next batch of hyper-marketed franchises (say, the sequel to the sequel to the spinoff of *Transformers 18*). This has especially unseated Australian films, which benefit from platform releases on a small number of screens before expanding as word of mouth spreads. Film scholar Karina Aveyard has noted that even successful titles like '*Lantana* (Lawrence, 2001) grossed $2.4 million in the first two weeks of its Australian cinema release but added almost three times as much to that total ($7 million) in the ten weeks of screenings that followed'.[10] Audiences seem to expect an extended period at the cinema, and seek endorsement from friends before seeing a local film that will invariably appear later on DVD or free-to-air television.

This scaling up can be seen everywhere, a point Steven Soderbergh made in his 2013 'State of Cinema' address to the San Francisco International Film Festival.[11] With the trend towards wider releases on more screens, it now costs around $30 million to release a film widely in the USA, and another $30 million to release in international markets, which now crucially account for 70 per cent of studio revenues. Because exhibitors will absorb around half of the box office, a studio will require at least $120 million in ticket sales to meet costs, and the bulk of profits will be made from a few big films and in the post-cinema markets. These economics clearly favour films with large budgets—after all, how many $15-million films are likely to take $120 million at the cinema, and how many distributors are willing to allocate a print-and-advertising budget that outweighs a film's entire production expenditure? A massively budgeted film, with all the sparkling stars and soundtracks and movie paraphernalia that can cross international media markets, is far more likely to succeed in this environment. So we can start to understand the effect this exponential scaling-up in distribution, and therefore production costs, is having on a small-to-medium-sized industry like Australia's, where the squeeze on screen space and budgets is already felt intensely.

The upshot is that not a single filmmaker or company has figured out how to distribute a film both widely *and* inexpensively, even with the near-revolutions in digital distribution. There is simply very little space or time for Australian films to screen, let alone find audiences, at the cinema. Instead, they are unavailable to mass audiences: buried beneath a mountain of intensely marketed *Marvel*-comic adaptations, and left to languish at small cinemas that are closing down by the year. This lack of accessibility contributes markedly to the widely held belief that Australian films are niche and elitist. It is not just the content of films that renders them unappealing to mass audiences, but their availability. The actions of distributors and exhibitors start shaping the public's attitudes to local films even before they are screened. Popularity cannot just be a function of storytelling and film content—distribution and accessibility do inform popularity. They are not the only factors that lead to popularity, but they are vital and, until now, hugely overlooked.

The third big-picture issue in the formal distribution sector is that cinemas are really designed to launch sales beyond the theatre—in DVD, online, TV, international and other supplementary markets. The empirical data in Figure 2 demonstrate that home-market sales have overtaken cinema-ticket receipts, a fact that Australian distributors do not take into sufficient consideration when devising release strategies. In the theatrical market, economically successful films are actually 'loss leaders' that break even only later in their post-theatrical afterlives. The largest distributors are vertically integrated subsidiaries of media companies that produce movies' extra-theatrical appendages. Their 'windowed'-release strategy depends upon tightly managed sequential and exclusive releases of different retail products at staggered intervals. Yet these further release windows and licensed platforms are usually absent from or under-exploited by Australian movies, which are effectively stand-alone productions with DVD and television licensing potentially managed by different companies. Only very rarely do local titles benefit from the spin-off merchandise, product placement, soundtracks, international sales and other ancillary products that make films profitable.

The cinema is no longer the key site for films. Only nine per cent of viewings take place in the cinema, and 65 per cent of viewings are on DVD/Blu-Ray. Online viewing of screen content is mainstream and on the rise,[12] thanks to the effortless accessibility of 'online viewing. [Viewers can] search [...] an almost infinite supply of screen stories [...] without leaving the comfort of their home.'[13]

Crucially, Australian films' DVD market share is routinely roughly double that of their cinema market share (see Figure 2)—an important point for understanding how local audiences are accessing film and for filmmakers and distributors to consider when asking how to expand audiences. Likewise, Screen Australia has consistently reported that lower-grossing local films tend to perform better on television than at the box office.

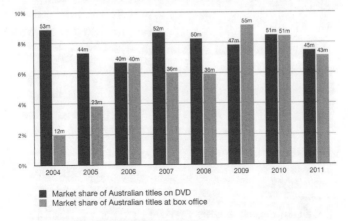

*Figure 2: Home market and box-office sales compared, 2004–11
Australian films are roughly twice as popular on DVD as at the
movies. Post-cinema distribution outlets open up availability of and
accessibility to films in a way not possible in the crowded theatrical
market.*

This could be because people watch on DVD and TV local films that they haven't already seen at the cinema. It could be that local titles are more readily available on television as a result of the regulated minimum level of local content: it is easier for distributors to sell local films to networks than it is to sell overseas titles that were more popular at the cinema. It could also be because different platforms are better suited to certain types of movies: the big screen for blockbusters and the home screen for 'smaller' films.

I detail the obstructions that Australian films face at the cinema not to whinge, but to show the necessity for energetic online and non-theatrical distribution. Ancillary markets are no longer ancillary, they are *the* markets. It is the cinema that is supplementary. However, we are yet to catch up with this reality:

Australian films are released stillborn into a theatrical system that is not designed for them and that therefore reduces their ability to compete. Small releases in art-house cinemas send the message that local films are old-fashioned and lack broad appeal. And in the other, newer viewing sites, to which audiences are gravitating, Australian film is greatly under-represented.

Production in a vacuum: Screen Australia's policy black hole

That is the big picture: Australian films are cut off from the means of distribution, and distribution is the route to popular and financial success. How does Screen Australia fit into this picture? Screen Australia's recent policy turns have consisted almost entirely in efforts to boost production and development through direct investment and tax rebates for private investors. Relatively fewer efforts have been made to rethink marketing, distribution and exhibition. By way of distribution policy, Screen Australia offers funds for promotional materials at festivals and a multi-platform funding program for transmedia stories such as video games. There is also the sorely needed $200,000 Innovative Distribution Program set to expire in 2013, and plans to replace it have yet to be announced. The main problem is that non-theatrical, non-commercial distribution and exhibition are seen as peripheral to policy, despite the fact that, according to Screen

Australia's own statistics, audiences are more likely to see an Australian film in the post-theatrical market than at the cinema.

How does distribution fit into Screen Australia's regular film funding? Feature-film funding and the Producer Offset guidelines require the involvement—'market attachment'—of a theatrical distribution company to provide both a massive injection of production funds and release the film into the market upon completion. This prerequisite precludes films that are signed with non-traditional distributors who are part of Screen Australia's Innovative Distribution program—an obvious policy contradiction that is yet to be resolved. It hands a disproportionate level of control to distributors who, despite their expertise, are innately conservative and risk-averse in predicting audiences' desires.

For a platform-neutral, market-attachment package

A more appropriate policy would enforce a platform-neutral, market-attachment package that places equal emphasis on non-theatrical avenues. Distribution is necessary and, indeed, should still be required, and by broadening the definition of market attachment from theatrical distribution to DVD, video-on-demand or non-theatrical, alternative distribution, the distribution of small-budget releases would be diversified in circuits to which viewers are gravitating. The main argument for retaining the current theatrical requirement is that cinemas give Australian films the best first chance in the market,[14] but this is becoming harder to maintain: 2013 has seen footy drama *Blinder,* cricket bromance *Save Your Legs!,* rom-com *Goddess* and surf movie *Drift* sadly underperform amidst a torrent of better-marketed releases. A poor box-office performance can unfairly and prematurely see a film labelled a dud.

The question of changing the currently compulsory theatrical release is not a peripheral issue. There can be little doubt that Screen Australia's demand for a presale is leading to a homogenisation of Australian films presented at the cinema. Distributors want a safe property with an assured audience. Might compulsory market attachment lead to pragmatic decision-making in order to mitigate risk and crack a safe market? Almost definitely. Might this lead to a one-size-fits-all approach, to the green-lighting of stock-standard film scripts that already meet certain preconceived genre or audience requirements? Perhaps. Creating films for the market is one thing, but having distributors hold back the gates to Screen Australia funding—at the expense of alternative ways of reaching audiences, and at a time when local titles are being zombied through theatrical releases—is another. After all, distributors often get it wrong: most films, not just Australian ones, are financial disasters, and commercial distributors have not been able to guarantee audiences.

Likewise, the Producer Offset stipulation for a theatrical release is becoming increasingly untenable. This year, media and entertainment lawyer Ian Robertson proposed extending the 40 per cent Offset to feature films that air first on television.[15] This is exactly the kind of policy shift required: one that focuses on increasing access to screen content rather than simply generating more of that content.

The challenge for policymakers is to acknowledge that the Australian film industry is not limited to the production sector or the cinema. How to let films reach their distributive potential, how to increase audience access—these are the questions that must be foremost in our thinking.

Film: a distribution-led business

Policy doesn't have to be developed in this way, and elsewhere it isn't. See, for example, the British Film Institute (BFI), which a decade ago took an approach premised on the recognition that the film industry

> is a distribution-led business [...] The Hollywood studios' mathematics are simple: money spent on production is more than earned back in distribution, profits are taken and the balance is used to help finance the production and distribution of more films [...Yet] much of the British film industry has developed a serious production habit for the last 50 years.[16]

Most British films were being 'made in a vacuum completely disconnected from distribution', and to rectify this disconnect, the BFI introduced matching investment schemes for distributors who acquired British films; funds to promote British films once they entered the marketplace; training for a new layer of film-distribution specialists, and funds to support the global distribution of British films. Clearly, these policies cannot be transplanted directly, but the logic underlying them is well worth our considering, particularly so in view of Screen Australia's continued avoidance of distribution policy. Speaking on ABC TV's *7.30 Report* in 2008, Screen Australia's then-CEO Ruth Harley maintained that

> the distributors know their business, that they know what to spend on the release of any particular film and they know that because they've got an expectation of box office and an expectation of ancillary rights. So I'm not inclined to think that Screen Australia should meddle in that business model.[17]

The subtext here is that distribution does not warrant rigorous inquiry in the policy realm and should be left to the private sector. This directly contradicts Screen Australia's mandate to support 'the development, production, promotion and distribution of Australian screen content'. A wide chasm separates the complex reality of film distribution and Screen Australia's policies.

Harley's assertion that distribution should be a policy-free zone makes no sense in the context of a theatrical market with little room for local films and a vibrant non-theatrical mediascape in which audiences are clamouring for and sharing new screen content. Screen Australia could be a vital link between filmmakers, distributors and exhibitors, and it should consider self-distribution or non-theatrical distribution as valid release methods that would benefit from funding and assistance. Screen Australia should at the very least publish case studies of successful and imaginative distribution campaigns for other filmmakers to learn from, based on the outcomes of their own Innovative Distribution Program, which over the last three years has benefited a range of non-theatrical and digital distributors. In addition to this, we need a historical database detailing the nature and impact of previous dynamic and effective film distribution-and-marketing campaigns. These case studies would provide invaluable ideas and lessons for filmmakers and distributors, and extend distribution expertise around the industry.

Not only do distributors provide essential upfront funding for film production, but they elect where and on how many screens films are played, the season length, the cost of the DVD and the television broadcast. These are not minor decisions, they are *key* to the construction of audiences. Distributors are involved in script development, casting and other creative decisions usually imagined to be exclusive to the production sector. Thus, distributors influence public thirst for aesthetic trends, inform audiences' encounters with films and prescribe which audiences see which films, and feed, structure and curtail demand.

Taiwan's film industry has similar problems to Australia's—an influx of Hollywood product and marketing force, and a squeeze on screens for local content. A half-screen release has eased these pressures: a film that can't sustain a wide release will share an auditorium with another title, alternating screening times. This means exhibitors can share risk, pack out fewer sessions and have more time to build publicity and word of mouth. This may not work for us, but it is worth our attention.

Rather than leaving distribution to commercial distributors, might not an independent committee of distributors (theatrical and non-theatrical), publicists and expert policymakers advise on film projects, from pre-production onwards, on how to build market-attachment packages aimed at reaching increasingly dispersed audiences? This distribution advisory board would provide information and experience that right now is mostly in the private sector, create estimates of potential box-office and ancillary-market perfor-mance, suggest the best release platforms for titles in development, offer advice on marketing schemes, and generally be a source of concrete knowledge on industry innovation in forward-thinking distribution. This board might ensure that, rather than being left to distributors, extra-theatrical distribution and marketing are consid-ered in a comprehensive and integrated manner from pre-production onwards and with the closer involvement of Screen Australia.

Interestingly, some overseas film-funding bodies do function directly as distributors. The National Film Board of Canada streams its archive of domestic shorts and features online, with links to download-to-buy and DVD options to support monetised distribution. Its site is an online store that makes conveniently- and well-priced local content accessible on demand. More generally, it's seen that 'to the extent that Canadian feature films are viewed by Canadians, Canadian distributors are seen to be helping to meet the objectives of Canada's feature-film policy'.[18] It's also recognised that a locally owned and controlled sector is required to finance and deliver Canadian content effectively —what Australia has, by contrast, is a few boutique distributors. Canada's is quite a different way of thinking about film policy, and one from which we would do well to learn. *In other words, distributors are critical partners for us in stabilising and expanding Australia's film industry*—so let's make that a key aspect of the way in which we advance a new distribution model.

Let's consider another international contrast. While the USA's industry is distribution-led, Australia's is production-led. Hollywood's is vertically integrated with a consistent, in-house approach to production, distribution and exhibition; Australia's is highly fragmented between these three sectors. US studios develop slates of features that are disseminated through their subsidiary companies, to which these companies retain the rights; Australian films are often produced by one-off, autonomous companies. The benefit of industrial integration between production, distribution and exhibition goes beyond the financial: there are practical benefits that affect which audiences see which pictures and where. With a consolidated approach to production, distribution and marketing, it is easier to control release cycles, to nurture films that require word-of-mouth and specialty publicity campaigns, and there is less pressure to pull a film off screens after a short and unsatisfactory run. A greater degree of clout and a larger stash of bargaining chips come with this kind of overall integration.

By comparison, Australian producers have few ongoing ties with distributors (though this is slowly changing), making the tasks of raising investment, offsetting the risk of production and selling rights to domestic and international distributors infinitely more difficult. Funding agencies spend millions on film production, only to let films loose into a competitive marketplace with virtually no support for effective distribution. The result is a random, inactive approach to distribution, with responsibility placed mostly on the shoulders of commercial distributors.

With this knowledge in mind, simply escalating production funding or simply changing the *kinds* of stories told will only cause filmmakers to stumble from one short-term expedient to the next.

2: The anatomy of a successful theatrical release

In light of the economic and policy realities outlined above, to suggest that all a film need do is tell a good tale, is, to say the least, fanciful. We've been asking the wrong questions. So instead of asking how we can change the kinds of films being made, or increase their production funding, I want to ask how local films can reach their distributive potential and which films are best suited to which audiences and which platforms. Let's start by asking what it is exactly that makes a film suitable for theatrical release.

Kriv Stenders' crowd-pleasing *Red Dog* (2011, $21m box office) was a family movie that appealed to a wide demographic: women and their partners, parents and grandparents bringing their little ones, and general viewers. Its marketing approach hinged on humour and Koko the dog. Roadshow, the distributor, undertook in-house marketing and started early, releasing a teaser trailer that went viral on YouTube. On the film's release, Roadshow toured Koko around the country and targeted not only families but veterinarians, animal charities and pet shelters. In addition to special charity screenings for shelters, the wide cinema release (on 270 screens) during school holidays triggered a range of flow-on products from merchandise to soundtracks in non-theatrical markets. Beyond the cinema, the film had an upbeat soundtrack and a DVD that was released in time for Christmas 2011—another shot aimed at the family market. It went on to become the biggest-selling Australian DVD of all time. In short, this was a very active distribution strategy with a well-considered use of marketing dollars. It ticked all the boxes of a theatrical release.

Similarly, Wayne Blair's *The Sapphires* (2012, $18m box office) was a musical that appealed to women, fans of the original stage play, fans of the band and soul music and general viewers. Made by Indigenous film-makers and intended for all audiences, its marketing campaign, focussed on the stars and the music, was launched at the Cannes Film Festival and utilised its local cast in musical performances that were well suited to radio and television. It capitalised on its stars' online media presence to the point where the Twitter page of its singer/actor star, Jessica Mauboy, retained the official promo image as its background and the phrase '*The Sapphires' Soundtrack available now*' as its by-line and a URL for over a year following the original release. This kind of direct celebrity-to-audience communication-as-marketing—Mauboy has 100,000 Twitter followers—is pure gold, but it requires a considered approach to the digital sphere by distributors. The film's wide release (on 275 screens) launched a number of post-cinema elements, including pay-TV and a soundtrack with Sony Music that has reached platinum sales. The film was pitched at an overseas market via a UK release hinged on the BFI London Film Festival and its Irish lead actor, Chris O'Dowd, a small-scale US release that played successfully on the suggestion that *The Sapphires* was an Australian *Dreamgirls* girl group. In other words, *The Sapphires* was not just a fun, Friday-night movie, but had a marketable soundtrack combining nostalgia (1970s soul music) and twenty-first-century commercial cool (an Australian Idol alumnus), deliberately honed internet buzz, a purposeful orientation to the home market, and appeals to more than one demographic quadrant.

There's a pattern to these successes, and it's not simply to do with pleasing a crowd. All the films have had wide releases, reasonable production *and* marketing budgets, DVDs with well-considered extra material and a well-timed release date, a partnered and cashed-up approach to marketing and the conscious mobilisation of several demographic quadrants. Moreover, most are adaptations and they bring with them pre-existing audiences. They are not stand-alone movies, but part of a longer chain of movie-related products, like soundtracks, which the cinema merely launches. They actively use the cinema to open up accessibility later down the track: television screens and DVDs can accommodate larger audiences than exhibition infrastructure. They satisfy the criteria for a theatrical release.

Successful films, failed release strategies

Films like these were well-equipped to perform in the formal distribution system; but there have been many more successful Australian films whose release strategies failed. *Save Your Legs!* (2013) had many supposed ingredients for box-office success: proven stars, a fun genre that Australianised *The Hangover* in many ways, a sporting theme, and its warm critical reception is typified by the *Sunday Age*'s Ed Gibbs, who called it 'authentic and endearing [...], an infectiously feel-good story that's accessible to all'.[19] It featured familiar and popular talent, Stephen Curry and Brendan Cowell, as man-boys for whom adulthood has fallen through. Their D-grade cricket team's tour through India brings them up against Indian management, the unreality of their sports-star dreams and the reality of grown-up responsibilities of career and family. The film is bromantic, blokey, light-hearted and nostalgic, albeit unambitious and tonally diverse, with the kind of upbeat feel that critics say audiences crave.

The film *should* have been a hit. But its release took little account of non-theatrical platforms like special-edition DVDs, digital delivery and soundtracks. In terms of marketing, the distributor couldn't import a ready-made publicity campaign from abroad, and failed to effectively construct their own, despite a hefty $1 million print-and-advertising budget. It is not a question here of the *amount* of the marketing budget, but of the *kind* of marketing needed to find an audience. There was little sustained use of low-cost or online strategies to build word of mouth, and insufficient effort to exploit its Australian cast during promotion. What audiences were offered was fairly standard: a promotional segment on Channel Nine's *The Cricket Show* and a competition offering a trip to India made available by a couple of online magazines. Its campaign suffered from the same cross-genre split personality as the film, which the poster illustrated perfectly: a broad comedy in the vein of *Kenny*, a matey Judd Apatow-style bromance, or an Australian-Bollywood sporting flick aimed at 'Nice Cricket-Obsessed Aussie Blokes'? Who exactly *were* the target audience? It wasn't apparent from the promotional material. To top it off, the film was released in the same week as the Wachowskis' multi-million-dollar epic *Cloud Atlas*, Steven Soderbergh's *Side Effects* and British rom-com *I Give It a Year*, all of them big-time, cashed-up, marketable films with all-star casts and imported publicity machines. All in all, *Save Your Legs!* failed to ask how best to engage its audience and contented itself with an unimaginative, cookie-cutter drive.

Myriad other local films have followed this failed release formula: rave-reviewed horror *100 Bloody Acres* (2013) is the latest—how on earth can a film with a tiny print-and-advertising budget, opening in six art-houses, be expected to compete? Low-budget thriller *Wasted on the Young* (2010), teen horror *The Loved Ones* (2009) and the Spierig brothers' all-star vampire sci-fi movie, *Daybreakers* (2009) are other examples. Their problem was not their stories. They all had the necessary ingredients for box-office success, but they relied on barely visible, auto-piloted releases. They are films that did not select the distributive circuits their audiences favour, and that failed to consider DVD and online arenas as much as theatrical ones. By looking at Australian films through the lens of distribution, the lesson is that those who view the theatre as the main arena of audience engagement and fail to factor in multiple channels of distribution are the most likely to fail to reach their distributive potential. Most of all it shows that a good story, a crowd-pleasing genre and even a marquee cast are not necessarily enough. A snappy distribution plan can't save a bad film. But distribution and marketing can make or break a good one.

The idea of a commercial, theatrical release, with its prestige, cultural legitimacy, immersive experience, big screen and booming sound, is seductive for filmmakers. But there are different audiences for different films, and that means different release strategies. Some films are better suited to touring, event-style releases with short, sharp publicity campaigns in regional and major cities, and involving key cast and crew. That kind of gig-like release, in which a film runs for a short season and local press are systematically targeted, would have been perfect for *Save Your Legs!* and *100 Bloody Acres*. Not only is the cost of these kinds of releases far more realistic compared with traditional, scattergun print-and-advertising strategies (which don't seem to benefit local titles anyway), they can pave the promotional way for an earlier DVD/VOD window.

Alternative, theatrical self-distribution

To show how small films can compete in the theatrical

system, let's turn to *Mrs Carey's Concert* by Bob Connolly and Sophie Raymond, a film that depended on an ABC licensing fee and Screen Australia's television-documentary fund rather than a distributor's pre-sale. In the directors' patient and unobtrusive style of observational filmmaking, the documentary follows Methodist Ladies' College Music Director Karen Carey as she prepares for the school's biennial Sydney Opera House performance. Mrs Carey is obsessive in her conviction that music is essential to education and character-building, and must gain the participation of every student in the school, from the high-achieving, self-doubting Emily to bad girl Iris. The film premiered at the Adelaide Film Festival on 28 April 2011 to considerable critical and audience acclaim. *Sydney Morning Herald* critic Sandra Hall wrote that, despite being a documentary, it was 'as spirited as any feel-good fantasy in the annals of the movie musical [...Y]ou must see the film, which is well worth every exhilarating minute.'[20]

Palace Cinemas, though not initially on board, approached the filmmakers to exhibit the movie following its festival success. But they rejected the distribution deal and instead organised their own nine-theatre release, which extended to 70 cinemas over 17 weeks as the word of mouth reverberated. They sold DVDs to audiences immediately after screenings as well as through their website. The result of this extensive distribution effort was a box-office tally of $1,158,281, with a total audience from cinema, DVD and television viewings amounting to 1.4 million, making it the fourth-highest-grossing, non-IMAX Australian documentary to date.[21]

The filmmakers, as distributors, knew their target audience and how to reach them. Co-director Sophie Raymond has confirmed that the self-distribution strategy worked

> because of the nature of the film. We met people who knew our audience, who had greater access to the audience, and no distribution company was going to have those classical music connections that we had developed. And in lots of ways that's what documentary people [...] think about, because they will be in a better position [than a distributor] to reach the people who are most passionate about whatever it is they're making.[22]

So the distribution process was a natural and creative extension of the production process, devised sensitively in a way that matched the film's style, content and target audience. The filmmakers and their publicist promoted the film systematically, personally and directly to the networks they had attracted during the production process, by inviting to screenings Sydney Symphony Orchestra tutors, for instance, and emailing members of the Australian Teachers of Media—40,000 of them—across the country.

Mrs Carey's Concert was able to strain against the limits of the current distribution system because it fulfilled the requirements of a theatrical release by mobilising a squarely identified audience who were willing to pay for cinema tickets: seniors, classical-music listeners, teachers and documentary lovers who, when given the option, prefer an Australian documentary to a foreign one. Cleverly, the filmmakers targeted the 'grey dollar': a cashed-up audience with a lifetime of habitual movie-going behind them.

The film's marketing drive tapped into its musical life, beginning with the BigPond Adelaide Film Festival, where, on opening night, its screening was followed by an orchestral performance. It then continued on AM radio with the release of a soundtrack featuring the MLC orchestra. The film launched a further cycle of releases on DVD, music and television. In this way, the theatrical release was a lighthouse attracting audiences to ancillary markets and participating in the community that was gathering around it.

Although self-distribution allowed the filmmakers to access ticket revenue directly, they could not bypass exhibitors' fees. Bob Connolly estimates that 75 per cent of the $1.2 million box-office gross was absorbed by exhibitors:[23] the filmmakers received 40-45 per cent of box-office sales in the first two weeks of the release, and this cut was reduced by 5 per cent each week until it reached 25 per cent.[24] So, ironically, the film's lengthy 17-week run was unusually advantageous for exhibitors and financially luckless for its producers. This is a standard exhibition deal, and it exposes yet another structural problem in the theatrical system. Exhibitors are the biggest beneficiaries of these long releases and the inability to short-circuit exhibitors' fees is an insurmountable limitation of the theatrical system. Connolly has declared that, although filmmakers make very little from self-distribution, conventional distribution yields them no financial return whatsoever.[25] This sentiment has been echoed by other filmmakers. For instance, Rachel Perkins has stated publicly that she 'has not seen a cent' of the $7.7 million netted by *Bran Nue Dae* at the box office.[26]

Mrs Carey's Concert shows that, given the right story and audience, self-distribution, commencing with, but not limited to, a theatrical release, is a viable option for local filmmakers. Within the confines of the theatrical system, a niche art-house film on a tight budget can actively generate an audience through a handmade, privately organised, informal distribution strategy. It would not suit all films, but those that have an audience who prefer the cinema and have a strong marketing hinge, such as musical content, should consider this kind of lo-fi, intensive, multi-pronged distribution approach.

3: Virtual theatres: moving the movies online

Now for the bigger media picture. The film industry is currently losing its mind over the insane circus of digital film and online distribution. Unlike video, the last major change in film distribution, peer-to-peer digital delivery does not merely add another window to the standard release cycle. It is a major, structural disruption of the distributive logic that informs how value is gained from film products. In the pre-digital period, ancillary markets simply comprised VHS and DVD rental and retail, cable television, free-to-air television and other supplementary spheres such as airlines. Business theorists have described how the major studios use this geospatial and temporal flow of products through pre-determined markets to control the value chain, extract profit and mitigate the costly and volatile nature of film production. Starting with their theatrical release, films move through these distribution markets or 'windows', taking years to complete the cycle throughout the world. The expensive nature of acetate film, the fundamental means of film production, allowed Hollywood to maintain tight control over every facet of its consumers' engagement with its subsidiary media companies. With the knowledge that few independent filmmakers could meet the cost of shooting, printing, editing and transporting acetate film, Hollywood has ensured its dominance abroad for the last ninety years.

With digitalisation, these release windows are no longer fixed, linear and sequential. The windows are in constant flux as products are cut from retail intermediaries like DVD stores and cinemas and shared between consumers, platforms and countries. This is at the heart of digital's disruption and the material dynamics underlying surface issues like file-sharing: the control, exclusivity and often arbitrary bottlenecks on which exhibitors and distributors have always depended have been shaken by the material shift from analogue to digital. Digital delivery has the potential to reorganise the production and consumption chain, bypassing the traditional gatekeepers of content, production studios, distributors and exhibitors, and granting filmmakers direct access to audiences and revenue. Already distributors have responded by shifting release windows. Global simultaneous film releases have moved from radical to commonplace as a way of pre-empting immediate cross-border file-sharing. Likewise, pay-per-view video-on-demand windows are opened at the same time as DVD releases. These are two practical ways in which digitalisation has impacted distribution and transformed release windows that were previously considered untouchable. The next development is the switch in theatres from analogue to digital cinema, and that is estimated to save the major studios alone around US$700-800 million a year.[27] The majors talk a lot about costs of unauthorised digital delivery, but scarcely ever about the savings of digital cinema.

Digital-rights management is another area in upheaval, and this has many unclear ramifications for making Australian content more widely accessible. The distributive systems of the analogue world cannot be simply carbon-copied onto the digital one. Many distributors continue to impose temporal and cost-based digital rights controls inflexibly on online distributors. For instance, certain films can be licensed under pay-per-view, but not subscription packages, some cannot be preceded by advertisements, others can. Although day-and-date VOD and DVD releases are now the norm, distributors are reluctant to apply this to subscription VOD releases, which follow a business model different from the Hollywood standard, in which each user pays for each individual film. This shows that the official channels are still figuring out how to transfer the distributive logic of the windowed system onto the digital world. A shift in rights management and a collapse of release windows to meet user demand would require an understanding that media businesses must now compete with the concept of 'free'—the abundance of free, quality, online content.

The rise of informal file-sharing, or piracy, is perceived by many in the film industry as an economic threat. From a distribution perspective, however, this is a highly efficient and accessible means of film dissemination, and it is potentially exciting for filmmakers. In their desire for content that is not at the mercy and timing of exhibitors and distributors, viewers are throwing formerly linear-prescribed windows into disarray; but when presented with inexpensive, convenient and legal downloading options, they readily embrace them. This is evidenced in the music industry by Apple's iTunes store, and in the USA, where the proliferation of affordable VOD sites has resulted in streaming overtaking physical carriers. Online dissemination and sharing could be seen less as a moral conundrum and more as an opportunity to reach wider audiences, provided other means of collecting revenue, merchandise, special edition DVDs and so on, are put in their place. Digitalisation makes the flow of content across different platforms inevitable, and presents filmmakers with an entire apparatus of windows that are open simultaneously. In some cases, filmmakers have even started to use pirates as distributors of their films—and profitably.

The Australian horror film *The Tunnel*, directed by Carlos Ledesma and driven by the team at Distracted Media, is perhaps the best example of this to date. Financed partly by crowd-funding, *The Tunnel* was one of the first films to benefit from informal methods of distribution as *the method* of distribution. Rather than fearing piracy, the filmmakers commandeered file-sharing to effectively reach their identified audience and drive interest in ancillary products. The film can be understood as an effort to unite emerging channels of film circulation into a financially sustainable template for future productions.

The Tunnel follows a news team as it investigates a secret, abandoned web of tunnels beneath Sydney's rail system. The film's tone leans away from 'slasher' towards that of a psychological thriller with a sense of home-grown authenticity and a lo-fi, low-budget horror aesthetic. Its cast are all unknown, as are its director and producers, but it was pitched at a decidedly active and devoted audience: horror fanatics. It premiered in Sydney on 18 May 2011 simultaneously online and on DVD and cable television. Though the film's limited theatrical run was by all means successful (its four Sydney screenings reached 60 per cent capacity, an enviable feat for any debut Australian feature), the main focus of the release strategy was elsewhere: authorised file-sharing, festivals, *Sydney Morning Herald* TV, ABC iView and an iPad application, which, all told, allowed the filmmakers to reach an estimated audience of four million.[28] (How these platforms were monetised will be outlined shortly.) *The Tunnel*'s multi-release approach contrasts sharply with the standard distribution of two (arguably better-quality) Australian films that were also released in May 2011: Justin Kurzel's *Snowtown*, which debuted on 16 screens and Brendan Fletcher's *Mad Bastards*, which opened on 27, before following the prescribed pattern of a DVD release several months down the track.

Peer-to-peer finance: *The Tunnel*'s crowd-funding strategy

The Tunnel's distribution strategy began well before its release with a crowd-funding effort in which members of the public were called on to donate $1—the imagined cost of one film frame—to reach a budget of $135,000 for a 90-minute film. By contrast, the bulk of films depend on a pre-sale from a distributor, which is then used to finance production and secure further investment. Richard Harris has described how

these media organisations—which have both committed money and also have access to the

audience—can insist on high levels of intervention in the process [...B]roadcasters and
distributors are rarely simply buying the best
ideas and projects from an independent community, but are almost always intimately involved
in the selection, development and production of
films and programs.[29]

Pitching to a distributor is considered a test of a project's
robustness. Films are unpredictable investments: they
are immensely costly and made with no guarantee
that a market exists for them. A distributor's role is to
mitigate the volatile nature of the market by selecting
films they predict audiences will want. In the peer-to-
peer economy, crowd-funding serves the same purpose.
Beyond providing finance, it demonstrates that there
is a desire among a broad range of consumers for such
a product. The investors of crowd-funded films are a
large network of audience members who use their own
money to see projects they want brought to completion. It is an extension of the same disruption of the
producer-consumer exchange impelled by peer-to-peer
music downloading software, Napster, over ten years
ago. Films that best exploit these new systems of peer-
to-peer financing are deliberately marketed from their
infancy to a distinct audience, a process that then shapes
the film's delivery and reception in active communities
of viewers. When a crowd-funded project is successful,
these investor-consumers become ambassadors of the
project, going on to purchase merchandise or other

ancillary products and forming a community of active fans. In the case of *The Tunnel*, audiences contributed just over $51,000 to its $135,000 budget. Rather than fully supplanting traditional funding partners, crowd-funding served the purpose of a pre-sale by proving the project's commercial viability and attracting other financial partners (i.e. Zapruder's Other Films and Screen NSW).

Crowd-funding stems from an expectation of authenticity in film culture: funders want to lend effective support to worthwhile projects that are overlooked by traditional investors. This assertion is supported by recent Australia Council research, which found that key motivations for crowd-funding participation are: knowing the creative team, emotional investment in belonging to a creative community, and forming an authentic connection to creative production.[30] These findings parallel those of an American study that found that donors value engagement with a trusted, creative and collaborative community and receive non-monetary validation in return for their contributions. The material incentives offered by filmmakers were cited as the least important reason for contributing.[31] *The Tunnel* is book-ended by two frames that thank supporters and ask for more financial support. This places a sense of responsibility and involvement in the project's success onto the audience. Supporters are also listed and thanked on a dedicated webpage.

The active crafting of a film's distribution strategies through participatory culture is vital. Audiences' concept of 'participation' has shifted. It used to mean purchasing a movie ticket, participating in the social space of the cinema and discussing a film with friends. Audiences now expect to interact more directly in a film's community and with its creators, as well as to construct and curate their own virtual theatres of films they care about. A gradual shift is occurring away from a 'provider' approach to cultural products towards greater participation and an increasingly two-way stream of *interaction* between user and producer. Of course, this audience activity is limited, but markedly more prominent than in the studio model. Crowd-funding does not level the field entirely. Crowd-funding filmmakers experience the same hardships as other independents: they cannot compete with the marketing might and ubiquity of the Hollywood product. Nonetheless, it shows that thoughtful approaches to distribution and financing can and should prioritise active audience engagement. In the case of *The Tunnel*, crowd-funding forced the filmmakers to foster a direct dialogue with audiences, and showed that an active and committed community of fans can help distribution.

Please seed: what digital distribution did for one small film

The key components of *The Tunnel*'s success as a self-distributed film were, first, the use of crowd-funding as a measure of audience demand; second, ease of entry for its filmmakers into the crowded film market and ease of access for audiences to view the film online; and third, marketing, particularly of social networking media, as an integral part of its release strategy to drive word of mouth.

Unhindered by box-office concerns and traditional gatekeepers like distributors, *The Tunnel*'s filmmakers were able to select distributive channels that would best lead them to their target audience. They emphasised globally available methods of release that were easily accessible for both the filmmakers as distributors and for audiences to view. The producers arranged partnerships with torrent sites to ensure their product was not lost in a sea of online offerings; unofficial downloads and streams are estimated at around three million. These figures reinforce file-sharing as a highly accessible means of film dissemination and audience engagement, while YouTube, *Sydney Morning Herald* TV, ABC iView and VODO provide ongoing income through licensing fees and advertising revenue.

The free download was used as a beacon for ancillary products sold through *The Tunnel* e-store, including digital downloads of the score, PDF eBooks, printable digital frames and autographed, limited runs of high-definition DVDs. The website also promotes an iPad application containing the same content as the DVD (i.e. the feature film with extras), available through Apple's iTunes store for less than ten dollars. All these channels (the online store, torrent and iPad app) are available internationally, rethinking what many see as a disadvantage, namely the Australian market's competition with other English-language cinemas. The final part of the film's release strategy was its sale to cable-television network Showtime and to Transmission Films for DVD retail in Australia and New Zealand. This shows that outsider efforts to build audiences through informal channels can lead to commercial success in formal circuits, and that some 'old world' media companies are open to shifting release windows.

Promotion: marketing as distribution, distribution as marketing

The Tunnel merged the arenas of distribution and marketing as entwined answers to the same question: how do we mobilise an audience? This question is compounded by the expansive nature of the web as a distributive form: the doorways to the online field are wide open, but the support and marketing required to influence consumers in that online space are largely absent. Not merely a promotional tool, *The Tunnel's* website was (and remains) an online store of ancillary products, and a mechanism that replaced the cinema as the key site of audience engagement. The film benefited from a handcrafted media strategy to combat being drowned in a tide of online products, aided by a public-ity firm and an online marketing strategist financed by a Screen NSW grant. The filmmakers argue that the labour and skills involved in such a concerted social media push would not have been possible without this grant, thereby strengthening the view that, despite much euphoria about the immediacy and free nature of social networking, Twitter and Facebook are time-consuming commitments but can be rewarding for the right projects. An emphasis on online outreach was appropriate for *The Tunnel*, as its core audience was young and internet-literate. A specialised, online presence can yield gains for producers who have the right audience and the funds and time to devote to this area.

The key question here for filmmakers of small and medium-sized films is this: without massive print and advertising budgets, how can wider layers of viewers be reached? *The Tunnel*'s producers saw file-sharing not as a shackle on the film industry, but as a means of free marketing: an effective, viral word-of-mouth generator. The film's innovative funding-and-distribution strategy became a cornerstone of the film's marketing scheme, and a type of free advertising in and of itself. Its filmmakers reached out with one hand to pro-piracy and horror fans on the net, and with the other to mainstream audiences, garnering coverage from publications like the *Sydney Morning Herald*, the *Daily Telegraph*, *Inside Film* and *Variety*. This coverage was less concerned with the film itself than with the idea that the filmmakers were attempting to solve some of the film industry's biggest problems by hijacking piracy and experimenting with audacious distribution and financing methods.

The Tunnel was a successful experiment in crafting a sustainable blueprint for film production out of disparate and emerging finance and circulation paradigms. Its crowd-funding technique was as much a generator of buzz as a source of finance, and is an excellent example of the way in which filmmakers are dissociating themselves from traditional intermediaries at early stages of production. Its free online launch was as much a promotion of supplementary products as a method of viral film release. The filmmakers' focus on ancillary markets led to more intensive and widespread distribution (that is, more distribution outlets). Unencumbered by box-office performance—which is increasingly irrelevant in the context of immense ancillary and informal markets—filmmakers can offer legal, audience-appropriate and inexpensive ways of viewing and sharing movies online not as a VOD afterthought, but as the centrepiece of their distribution strategy. Peer-to-peer networks made viewers key distributors of *The Tunnel*, increasing its distributive potential. By using a freely downloadable film and word of mouth to sell scarce goods (ancillary products), the filmmakers harvested an income and built demand for future projects.[32]

A second thriller, *Airlock*, is currently under development by the same production team, using the same financing and distribution framework. Thanks to the success of the original *Tunnel*, a sequel, entitled *The Tunnel: Dead End*, has secured Screen Australia funding, indicating that lo-fi, self-distribution can lead to funds and theatrical distribution for future projects. This suggests that this model is not a one-off experiment, but the basis for a professional body of work, and that a simultaneous, multi-platform release through peer-to-peer, DVD, Apple store and cable television, and in accordance with the varying ways that audiences access film, can meet consumer demand and enhance rather than limit independent filmmakers' revenue collection. Further, discarding the windowed system's artificial bottlenecks allows producers to recoup costs quickly, rather than by following the traditional release method and recovering investment over year-long cycles of staggered releases.

Download this movie: what can digital distribution do for local films?

Consumers have wrestled back some control over access to media products and are unlikely to relinquish it, as evidenced by the failure to contain peer-to-peer technologies. Research suggests that a strong correlation exists between piracy and paid media consumption: studies in Norway and the UK have shown that in the music industry, file-sharers are far more likely to purchase music than those who don't pirate, and similar findings apply to the online publishing and software industries.[33] What this means is that we must change our mindset, and begin to see the positive opportunities in digital, rather than the slings and arrows that it hurls. While digital doesn't mark the end of cinema, it may well mark the end of a business model that tries to contain and control an audience's interactions with films at every step of the consumption process. How can Australian filmmakers hijack peer-to-peer infrastructure to build a culture of local-movie appreciation, and add an Australian film habit to a Hollywood one? How can online and currently informal-viewing mechanisms be formalised into new approaches to distribution? The answers are not yet clear, but the questions must be asked.

While Australian films remain much less available than they might be to mainstream audiences at multiplexes, an examination of the online realm clearly demonstrates that local content has a greater chance of becoming popular when it is accessible. The abundance of self-distributed professional content on user-generated websites provides ample proof of this. These kinds of projects, such as *Bondi Hipsters* (2011–13), *Event Zero* (2012) and *One Step Closer to Home* (2011), can reach large audiences and generate income through branding, product placement and advertising revenue-share programs like YouTube Partners. Again, while they don't offer a full-replacement strategy for the theatre, they remain a sign of what lies around the corner. They have high production values and are driven by established film and television professionals working consistently in the emerging field of web-only content. They harness the effectiveness of informal user-led distribution and place no cost restrictions on users. In some cases, they are co-financed by formal structures. Where *The Tunnel* was an experiment in online film distribution, *Event*

Zero, by the same team, constitutes the next link in the chain in developing a professional body of work that is made to exist online, and the institutionalisation of a previously informal distribution channel: the web. We need to remain open to the ways digital can supplement traditional screen content and reach new audiences: monetisation is occurring through pay-per-view mechanisms too, not just advertising, as more distributors utilise YouTube as a video-on-demand provider.

Video-on-demand offers another glimpse of what can be done to engage wider layers of spectators through innovative distribution. As a way of experimenting with the potential for VOD beyond re-selling Hollywood content, VOD-provider Quickflix.com.au has proposed a branded, online film festival of emerging Australian filmmakers. Likewise, BeamAFilm.com provides carefully curated Australian and art-house titles neglected by formal channels and that, due to their cult status, are difficult to find even on informal file-sharing sites. Offering a thoughtfully programmed, inexpensive, differentiated online film-going experience that is unavailable elsewhere and therefore hard to imitate—this is the kind of forward-looking strategy we need, if we are to respond to the changing ways audiences are accessing films. Online curation—the authoritative recommendation of content to audiences—has much unexplored potential to cultivate a more active culture of Australian film-going online and at home. This is particularly pressing for Australian content, as much older content has not been digitised, and most formal

VOD providers seek merely to re-sell digital versions of Hollywood content already available at the cinema.

It can't be said often enough: we need, urgently, to amend the current definition of 'market attachment', and to move toward a distribution package that elevates VOD to the same level as theatrical. This will go some way towards breaking the distribution bottleneck on cinema screens and allow smaller online distributors to play in the space currently dominated by the theatrical companies. The future of subscription-based VOD distributors is still unclear: Netflix seems to have no Australian strategy, and no similar provider is leading the way. We need subscription, download-to-own providers that make Australian titles available. No wonder Australia has the highest piracy rates in the world, and its audiences have not fully embraced VOD—they've hardly been given the choice. Already, with the limited options on offer, the VOD and electronic sell-through market has grown 36 per cent year this past year and makes up more than ten per cent of the overall home-entertainment industry.[34]

We know that online and ancillary distribution doesn't yet totally fill the finance-and-revenue gap left by theatrical distributors, but we also know that pressure to remove theatrical distribution as the key trigger for funding, and therefore to fill that finance gap, will continue to mount. Until more concrete systems of distribution emerge, it will most likely be the state bodies that can trial flexible and responsive short-term policies, like ScreenWest's 3-for-1 crowd-funding matching fund, which tripled the funds pledged by fans for six projects in 2012–13.

4: Rethinking film distribution: ideas for new approaches

Mrs Carey's Concert and *The Tunnel* are not the only films to have successfully navigated the overarching cinema industry structures on their own terms and to have devised distribution strategies that actively connect them to their audiences.

If we turn to extra-theatrical distribution circuits, we see that large, if invisible, audiences do indeed exist for Australian films. There is a layer of films that neither employ the services of a distribution or exhibition company nor utilise the main metric of audience measurement: the box office. Aboriginal rights doco *Our Generation* (2010), animated comedy *Little Johnny the Movie* (2011) and queer documentary *Trans Boys* (2012) have all relied on screenings organised by filmmakers, fans or community groups. Films like counter-culture doco *This is Roller Derby* (2012) and therapy drama *Men's Group* (2008) were distributed through non-theatrical venues including RSL clubs and town halls. Beyond this quasi-theatrical layer, there's a growth in the use of digital-delivery mechanisms. Many film professionals use the advertising-supported online-distribution pathways offered by YouTube Partners and *Sydney Morning Herald TV*. There is also a growing rash of professionally produced, web-only screen content that exists entirely outside conventional theatrical and retail outlets and uses merchandise and advertising-supported business models. These include Distracted Media's thriller *Event Zero* (2012), pop-culture phenomenon *Bondi Hipsters* (2011–13), deadpan suburban satire *One Step Closer to Home* (2011), lesbian soapie *The Newtown Girls* (2010–11), rich-kid soap opera *SYD2030* (2012), vlog-style drama *Ozgirl* (2009) and meme-ish cartoon comedy *Beached Az* (2008, eventually screened and released on DVD by the ABC). Another example of highly effective and informal distribution, agriculture documentary *Growing Change* (2011) was sold primarily via USB drives and digital files ordered online and passed on from viewer to viewer, tapping into an expanding market of community gardeners and urban greenies. Melbourne's ACMI and Cinémathèque provide more doses of a cinema culture that can't be summed up by box-office reporting, as does Sydney's Kinema and Golden Age alternative theatres.

All this is proof that our film culture does not live in the motion-picture theatre, but the audiences utilising these other circuits are largely invisible because the mainstream media continues to measure Australian cinema solely according to box-office sales and ratings.

How to end the distribution scarcity

We've seen how the necessary machinery of hit-making

is not behind the bulk of Australian films. It makes a powerful case for looking beyond the theatrical horizon towards a 'handmade' approach to distribution and marketing that takes equal account of non-theatrical circuits. The goal of a handmade distribution approach is to grow audiences for local content, increase filmmakers' revenue share and refocus release strategies on the question of accessibility.

The scarcity of theatrical screens creates a space for enlarging digital distribution of local titles. Writes Richard Harris:

> There are concerns that the small number of Australian films released cannibalise each other's markets. Digital distribution could reduce pressure on the theatrical market; some films might not need theatrical release at all.[35]

As well as individual enterprise, wide-scale policy solutions are clearly needed to address the distribution sector's structural exclusion of local films. This would entail regulation, trade adjustments and industrial restructuring to break up what is currently a de facto vertically integrated system. Might tax incentives be made available to combined production/distribution enterprises, with the aim of integrating these two sectors? Might there be policy precedents abroad that have steered audiences toward local content? France's stringent quotas on foreign imports are famously effective. What about a minimum length of distribution for local films in cinemas, levelling the playing field for local titles and giving audiences more of a chance to choose a local title—a chance the crowded cinema market is making increasingly difficult. This policy warrants further investigation, particularly given our knowledge that local titles benefit from longer theatrical runs. The same precedent exists in television—the film industry's most stable sector—which is compelled by government regulation to broadcast local content in prime time. The fear is that any kind of proactive intervention will alienate cinemas. Naturally, exhibitors can be expected to cry out against any kind of regulation, but we need policies that go beyond pragmatism—this is the type of measure that would allow local films the time to accrue word of mouth and build larger audiences. After all, the aim of this policy is to increase ticket sales.

For too long Australia has been too hesitant about pointing out these big-picture policy-support mechanisms, as though intervention and regulation—in the context of heavy-duty monopolisation of the distribution-and-exhibition architecture—somehow disable the possibility of a commercial local film industry aimed at the wide public. What we need in the long term is to restructure the industry towards a distribution-led approach to production. As a first step, we need to shake up our distribution model so as not to fall totally behind the digital shift—we are already several steps behind the audience.

This essay also proposes a toolkit, drawn from the most effective existing experiments in lo-fi distribution, for filmmakers to tactically navigate their way through the existing apparatus on their own terms.

Both *The Tunnel* and *Mrs Carey's Concert* point to the possibility of an enlarged role for filmmakers in distribution, as a natural extension of the production process. Both demonstrate the way in which cinemas are but a single means by which audiences view screen content, and that marketing and distribution are indivisible. Both films demonstrate the enormous, often overlooked ability of Australian films to build a direct relationship with local audiences. And finally, both films are charged with a sense of possibility: rather than sleepwalking through their releases, the filmmakers saw distribution as a way of creating the film culture they regard as possible and necessary. Rather than changing narrative styles while working within the existing budgetary and distribution constraints, in both cases active audiences were encouraged to contribute to the kind of film culture they desired and to get behind the distribution process.

A handmade distribution model comprises four features.

- First, employing a publicist who specialises in film distribution, to supply the experience and networks usually provided by a distributor.

- Second, addressing niche markets through low-cost strategies and innovative marketing, in an effort to inventively mobilise audiences within the confines of small print-and-advertising budgets.

- Third, building one-on-one relationships with exhibitors to schedule a film's release sensitively.

- Fourth, by using a number of different distribution circuits, rather than *just* the theatre, you can reach beyond the exhibition infrastructure to maximise audiences.

Let us look more closely at each of these in turn.

1. A specialist publicist

The first essential component of a handmade model of distribution is to employ a publicist who specialises in the distribution of independent film and has the expertise to craft a DIY marketing campaign that combines traditional print-and-advertising with social-media campaigning. The traditional tasks of a publicist are to book interviews, craft a coherent public message and liaise with media. *Mrs Carey's Concert* employed publicist Kim Lewis, who is also a freelance cinema programmer, and had working relationships with independent cinemas. Likewise, *The Tunnel* employed consultant Thomas Mai, who advised on the use of the film's website as a central distributive channel.

The complex nature of the film industry necessitates a highly specialised division of labour. Traditionally, distributors and sales agents possess skills and knowledge that filmmakers need but don't have. They have pre-established relations with exhibitors and advertisers, and the expertise to mitigate the erratic nature of the film business and cut through the marketplace to mobilise a film's target audience. Hence, in a handmade-distribution strategy dissociated from the major intermediaries, the specialist publicist steps in to supply the experience and networks usually provided by a distributor.

2. Activating niche audiences through low-cost marketing

The next factor in handmade distribution is the need to address niche markets through low-cost marketing schemes. This is the job of the publicist. Here, the term 'low-cost' is relative to the cost of signing with a distribution company and will likely require the involvement of traditional funding sources in the form of private or state investment.

The particulars of these low-cost strategies are necessarily unique to each film, but might include traditional media campaigns and movie promotions such as two-for-one offers and ticket giveaways through newspapers and film magazines. Online outlets offer the opportunity for precisely identified low-cost strategies: targeting online 'what's on' magazine-style websites for write-ups and ticket competitions, and special deals for users of a film's Facebook page can encourage positive word of mouth in localised, specific circles of viewers.

For *Mrs Carey's Concert*'s preview screenings, special invitations were issued to leading members of the film's target audience, as well as the usual media cohort. Special public launch screenings were held in capital cities with filmmaker Q&A sessions (cited by the co-director as an important drawcard for audience members) and preceded by an intensive two- or three-day local-media campaign, enabling a direct conversation between filmmakers and audience. In the case of *The Tunnel*, a young, technologically literate audience was activated through inventive online marketing. A couple of examples: the names of the first twelve-hundred crowd funders were incorporated into the film's poster design, and the poster was spread across social-media websites and blogs. Another example was the gifting of DVDs at the theatrical premiere to people who tagged *The Tunnel* on Facebook.

3. Liaising with exhibitors to schedule release times

The third component is to talk with exhibitors face-to-face in order to execute the film's release in a manner congruent with its key audience. The most successful independent cinemas are familiar with the viewing desires and habits of their constituencies and can program events and theatrical runs accordingly. As evidenced by Kim Lewis, experienced film bookers/ publicists can work with cinema owners to negotiate screen time, program the most appropriate session times, negotiate splits and trailer placements, and monitor a film's performance. Building relationships with individual cinemas ensures that local films are released to local audiences in a networked and supported way. This goes some way towards bridging the gap left by traditional distributors, who have a monopoly on these kinds of professional relationships. Through self-distributing, Bob Connolly became familiar with the particulars of Sydney's film market:

> Cremorne Orpheum, for example, was doing exceptionally well [...] but then Roseville Cinema wanted the film. [Our publicist] said, 'No, you can't have it, you have to wait. If Roseville take it, that's going to eat into Orpheum. And they'll get angry and they'll go down. So you'll just have to wait your turn.' And they did, they waited about a month and then they put it on.[36]

Likewise, Rachel Lucas' self-distributed *Bondi Tsunami* (2004) targeted cinemas along the Eastern coast during summer holidays with the aim of selling DVDs, as did Serhat Caradee's ethnic-crime drama *Cedar Boys* (2009) in Sydney's west. These are all instructive examples of filmmakers making the best of the limitations of the theatrical system.

When it comes to reaching a film's target audience, timing is as vital as minimising conflict with other films and locations that may split the audience. Thinking creatively about further release cycles can also extend a film's extra-theatrical performance. For instance, re-releases of DVDs and special packages of bundled merchandise (e.g. a director's cut, poster, film stills, digital soundtrack and so on) can be promoted around key calendar dates such as Mother's Day and Christmas. With *Mrs Carey's Concert*, the value of extra-theatrical distribution circuits and live events that are built around the film's musical and its associated products sequences was vital: live performances, AM radio airplay, and screenings at 22 festivals in total. Likewise, *The Tunnel* had an extension of events designed to build an active community: a presence at horror-film festivals, and a premiere that was pitched to film professionals and fans as much as to the media ('Be a part of film history as we unleash a new breed of filmmaking upon the globe—and find out how YOU can do it too'). Tickets were made available to the public, and after the film's screening the production team answered the audience's questions.

4. Using simultaneous and concurrent distribution channels

The last major step is day-and-date releasing, exploiting numerous and concurrent distribution circuits.

A handmade strategy counteracts the fragmentation of the media landscape by bringing together the various disparate methods of dissemination—theatrical, VOD, television, and DVD—into a considered release plan, including informal release mechanisms like self-organised screenings outside the multiplex/art-house template, and/or formerly unauthorised digital realms. This formal-informal interface is particularly important in the context of a mediascape fractured along multiple lines of consumption. For instance, the filmmakers of *Mrs Carey's Concert* sold DVDs alongside their self-administered theatrical screenings, and also signed a separate deal with a DVD distributor to reach a wider audience through retail outlets in Australia and New Zealand.

This includes informal release mechanisms such as self-organised screenings outside multiplexes and art-houses and/or formerly unauthorised digital realms. For the makers of *Mrs Carey's Concert*, ancillary markets were a primary focus:

> [The] sole objective of [the theatrical release] is a DVD sale. That's what this is for. If you want to [...] bask in the limelight with a theatrical release, which every film would like, that's fine, but it's the DVD release [that will be financially successful]. When you give a film to a theatrical distributor, they will take the DVD rights for exactly the same reason.[37]

For this reason, the filmmakers retained the rights to the sale of DVDs and musical merchandise from their own website, as well as selling DVDs through Madman's retail partners.

Handmade self-distribution does not fundamentally alter the structural power relationships between Hollywood and Australia's local industry but it can be taken on immediately by filmmakers in the current transitional period of digital transformation. While neither *The Tunnel* nor *Mrs Carey's Concert* proposes an entire reorganisation of the theatrical system, they both reshuffle the relationship between filmmakers and theatrical intermediaries, engaging tactically with the most useful parts of the existing institutions without being circumscribed by them. In other words, instead of replacing traditional revenue systems totally, filmmakers can employ handmade self-distribution tactics.

Other future directions

In what new ways might these alternate release models bolster, instead of undermine, a film's opening weekend? Might some films be made available before they hit the cinema? VOD sneak previews could be a great way to pitch films at prospective audiences and, stressing exclusivity and choice factors—'See *Wolf Creek 2* before it's in theatres', or 'See the film the way YOU want to!'—ratchet up word of mouth immediately prior to release. It's neither as far out or as far away as it might seem: Magnet Releasing in the US is having considerable success letting platform-release-style films loose into VOD before theatres.

Perhaps the next innovation in distribution will be a simultaneous theatrical and DVD release. Might audiences be able to buy the DVD in the foyer, immediately after seeing a film, and get a discount if they produce their ticket stub? Let's pre-empt the pirates by opening up monetised streams of content. Closing the cinema-to-DVD window would provide audiences with convenient, inexpensive, legal options for take-home movies, and return revenues to producers more quickly.

The pressure on us to embrace day-and-date releasing wholeheartedly and promptly across VOD, theatrical and DVD will continue to mount. Indeed, the windows have already morphed. Providing legal, convenient methods of access is the only way to challenge piracy. Many distributors are behind day-and-date, and there are a range of incentives to exhibitors (and audiences) that could bring them on board. For example, say *Wolf Creek 2* is showing at your local cinema. What if a live Q&A with the director and stars were beamed immediately afterwards onto the screen via satellite? What if viewers tweeted questions and made the experience interactive? What if a vlog or podcast of the event were made available the next day? This would go far beyond the usual $20 movie-and-popcorn experience. US director Kevin Smith did something similar, and very profitably, with his horror movie *Red State* (2011): distributed day-and-date across VOD, DVD and theatres by Lionsgate. Such is the audience-expanding potential of digital cinema projection—selling tickets, not to films, but to events and theatres, giving fans the chance to buy a unique experience.

Day-and-date also opens up the possibility of inexpensive marketing measures that connect filmmakers with fans. To launch their indie comedy *Sleepwalk With Me* (2012) on VOD, Ira Glass and Mike Birbiglia asked fans to hold pizza/viewing parties at home on the same night, and dropped into as many homes as they could via Skype to say, 'Hi, thank you. What do you think of our movie?' It goes to show how—once we acknowledge that the theatrical window has already shrunk—engaging with fans might be opened up in extraordinary ways.

5: The future of the cinema

A flourishing local film industry needs functional distribution channels. Beyond the handmade model of tailored distribution for small-to-medium-sized films just set out, we must consider what an alternative national distribution policy and network might look like. We need to assess how Australian films relate to popular consumption sites, not just the cinema, and in this light to re-consider potential audience-engagement strategies.

The advent of digital delivery has given rise to the fear that cinema is in decline. Cinemas hold optimal viewing conditions not available at home: surround sound, a huge screen and 3D. But beyond these technological attractions, the attachment of audiences and filmmakers to the cinema lies elsewhere. Movie-going is a holistic and social experience enjoyed with others. Screen Australia's research shows that, when asked why they go to the movies, 'more than half [of respondents] agreed that the "cinema ambience", "big screen", [and] "relaxation" [...] were reasons [...] When asked to identify the single most important reason, "socialising" topped the list, followed by "tagged along' with others"'.[38] These social motivations show that it is not just mesmerising content that draws audiences, but mesmerising experiences, and it is here that the heart of the cinema's durability lies. The value and popularity of films is not falling; on the contrary, Australians are among the keenest film-goers in the world, and the box-office gross has scaled $1 billion every year since 2009.[39] Despite the protestations of the major studios, the statistics tell us that cinema-going is more popular and profitable today than ever before.

Some may be critical of elevating digital delivery to the level of theatrical release, and of treating local films as freebies in order to stimulate sales of affiliated merchandise and DVDs. A theatrical release, however, is a loss leader that is most economically effective when it launches downstream products. Furthermore, a freebie is ineffective in reaching large audiences for local titles, and is profoundly unprofitable for filmmakers and investors who see the bulk of ticket sales absorbed by exhibitors and distributors. Online distribution and the encouragement of a local film culture are complementary, not mutually exclusive, goals. This notion is supported by Screen Australia research, which has found that, far from replacing them, digital delivery is *supplementing* cinema and traditional viewing sites.[40]

What then does the future of the cinema look like? We are seeing cinemas become permanent sites of film festivals angled at particular niche audiences. The popularity of film festivals has increased substantially in the last ten years, providing a counter-parallel to the decline of independent cinemas. In 2001, there were 31 film festivals operating across Australia; that number now tallies 103, including three online/mobile festivals. The gap left by shuttered independent cinemas is being partly filled by the growth of film festivals, a popular outlet for Australian titles. This shows a healthy interest in non-Hollywood films, despite the closure of the cinemas that service them.

In other words, the function of the cinema is not dying, just changing. Festivals are an essential component of many local releases, as Adelaide Film Festival's Katrina Sedgwick acknowledges:

> Art-house Australian films can really struggle to get audiences, and yet in the context of our festivals, Australian titles that we world-premiere are almost always the first to sell out [... T]here are quite a number of very good films that can't survive [in the theatrical distribution system.]

We've all worked very, very hard to develop strong and loyal audience bases, and they're also people who are active participants in film culture [...] Our average audience member comes and sees eight films, so we're talking about committed people to film culture.[41]

This is the strongest empirical argument challenging the assertion that Australian films are unpopular. When targeted at the right audiences and made available through appropriate distributive channels, they perform very well indeed. The question is how to mobilise this audience *between* film festivals. There is still some way to go in terms of supporting follow-through distribution after the festival circuit. A platform-neutral market-attachment package that diversifies the distribution of art-house films in circuits popular with audiences— such as was outlined earlier—would go a long way to answering this question. There's much more potential here. Might Screen Australia sponsor streams of new Australian films in the major festivals, films that are not suitable for commercial release, but that would find an enthusiastic, niche festival audience? Might assured festival release qualify as a type of market attachment?

The anti-multiplex

Independent cinemas have two enormous advantages over multiplexes: curatorial authority, and the ability to form relationships with their local audience by crafting varied and flexible programs. There are a number of independent cinemas that do this very successfully. For instance, the Hayden Orpheum in Cremorne, Sydney, has a wide program outside its new-release schedule, which includes classics, non-cinematic material such as opera, ballet and National Theatre Live broadcasts, as well as special Q&A events with filmmakers, critics and media personalities. It's a beautiful venue in which to see movies and socialise: it understands that film culture is more than just the movies themselves. This curatorial and localised differentiation from the multiplex is the core of their business model.

Producer Robert Connolly's Cinema Plus presents a select number of special-event theatrical screenings of new local films around the country for films like *The Turning* (2013). Earlier this year, despite having premiered it on free-to-air television to 1.3 million viewers, Cinema Plus screened the teledrama, *Underground: The Julian Assange Story* (2012), to sell-out audiences in Sydney, Melbourne, Canberra and elsewhere. These events were accompanied by value-added components: interactive talks with Assange's mother, filmmakers and key talent from the film and directing-the-actor workshops. Audiences also received free CD-ROMs of bonus content: the screenplay, commentary, featurettes, stills. This shows that the approaches taken by *The Tunnel* and *Mrs Carey's Concert* were far from being flukes. Engaging tactically with the cinema space by means of DIY event-style runs and a constellation of media moments can build a direct line of communication with audiences and promote ticket sales and ancillary products. Artistically, this approach can build a context for the film and a memorable experience unavailable to home viewers or at a regular screening. The big multiplex chains just don't offer this kind of experience.

While the fragmentation of films throughout media outlets and platforms has led to audiences engaging with the movies they love in a markedly different way, the physical experience of going to the cinema is not a thing of the past. By enhancing the distinctly cinematic and experiential aspects of movie-going (optimal viewing conditions, intelligently curated programs) and sometimes combining them with live events, exhibitors can ensure that online consumption continues to grow the desire for cinema rather than replace it.

6: Conclusion

This essay is just one contribution to, and certainly not the final word on, a dialogue about the role of distribution in bringing Australian film out of the cul-de-sac in which it currently finds itself. Some of the ideas expressed here may already be out of date. So I emphasise the pressing need to re-think distribution as the vital way in which we conceive and reach out to our audience—and an urgent problem requiring a solution for Australian filmmakers. We can no longer afford to define our film industry as the production sector and sideline distribution, marketing and exhibition.

I hope that my main point—that a production-led approach to film funding and policy will never give us the sustainable industry we need and deserve—will generate lively discussion. An industry hooked on an addiction to production and development will always remain cut off from the market. The numbers are face-punchingly straightforward: finance is spent in production and regained in distribution. The box office is simply not where audiences are gravitating: online and ancillary markets are the real markets. Without that link to distribution, we will float adrift from the audience and the means of self-sustainability.

Let me end by noting the symmetry in the innova-tions currently ripping up the old film-distribution paradigms and the previous stretches of upturn for Australia's film industry: between the period leading up to 1920 and the renaissance in the 1970s and 80s that resulted in a new wave of 'Ozploitation' films. Australia's early cinema period was characterised by myriad experi-mental exhibition practices—cinemas in converted shopfronts, rooftops and open-air squares—that were inexpensive and adaptive to spectators. Likewise, Mark Hartley's documentary *Not Quite Hollywood: The Wild, Untold Story of Ozploitation!* (2008) contains first-hand accounts by filmmakers of an ad hoc and energetic attitude to film production that resulted in the crea-tion of a new audience for a range of films outside the mainstream film culture. George Miller called it 'gonzo filmmaking'. This outside-the-box and sometimes anarchic sensibility has much the same sense of possibility as the self-styled distribution efforts of *Mrs Carey's Concert* and *The Tunnel*, and offers alternative notions of distribution that enable filmmakers to fill gaps in the market. An audacious, flexible and technologically discerning mindset allowed these filmmakers to look beyond the horizon line of the staid theatrical system and astutely to seek out their own audiences.

Glossary

Day-and-date, a film's simultaneous release in cinemas, on DVD and online.

Event-style, a film's screening with key cast-members present and extra activities, such as a Q&A with the director, that are unavailable at a regular cinema screening.

P2P, peer-to-peer, a method of digital file-sharing that allows media to be directly shared between consumers freely and without authorisation.

Release windows, the various media markets—cinema, DVD, television etc.—through which a film's release is staggered, in order that it may recoup its costs in multiple areas over a long period of time, not just during the theatrical release.

Types of release:

Platform release, a film's initial release on a small number of screens prior to release on a greater number of screens.

Limited release, a film being supplied to cinemas in fewer than 100 prints. Most Australian films fall into this category.

Mainstream release, refers to a film being supplied to cinemas in 100-199 prints. Films from India/UK/France dominate this category.

Wide release, films being supplied to cinemas in 200-399 prints. US films dominate this category.

Blockbuster release, films being supplied to cinemas in 400 prints and more. US films dominate this category.

VOD, video-on-demand, an online viewing mechanism.

Endnotes

1. Garry Maddox, 'Movie Investors Wait for a Glittering Prize', *Sun Herald*, 4 November 2012, http://www.smh. com.au/entertainment/movies/movie-investors-face-wait-for-a-glittering-prize-20121103-28qug.html (accessed 23 July 2013).

2. Screen Australia, 'What to Watch: Audience Motivations in a Multi-screen World', June 2012, http://www. screenaustralia.gov.au/getmedia/4972fa65-caa5-4235-86be-1800e4a2815b/Rpt_WhattoWatch.pdf (accessed 26 August 2013).

3. See, for example, Richard Harris, *Film in the Age of Digital Distribution: The Challenge for Australian Content*, Platform Papers, no.12 (Sydney: Currency House), p.63.

4. 'Digital' refers here to new delivery channels such as video-on-demand, streaming, user-generated and peer-to-peer platforms, and also more broadly to ways of doing and thinking in the film industry that were not possible before the internet, such as crowd-funding.

5. Graham Shirley, 'Australian Cinema: 1896 to the Renaissance', in *Australian Cinema*, ed. by S. Murray (Sydney: Australian Film Commission, 1994), p.5.

6. Ross Jones, *Developments in the Cinema Distribution and Exhibition Industry*, report to the Australian Competition and Consumer Commission, 31 March 1998, http://www. accc.gov.au/content/item.phtml?itemId=305272&node Id=9b0ec153ed33f24f539b5f95d43436d5&fn=The%20 Cinema%20Industry.pdf, p.33 (accessed 27 May 2013).

7. Australian Film Commission, *The First Wave of Australian*

Feature-Film Production: From Early Promise to Fading Hopes, industry report, 2005, http://afcarchive.screenaustralia.gov.au/downloads/policies/early%20history_final1.pdf, p.5 (accessed 27 May 2013).

8. Jon Silver & Frank Alpert, 'Digital Dawn: A Revolution in Movie Distribution?', *Business Horizons*, 46.5 (2003), pp.57-66. (p.5).

9. Screen Australia, 'Number of Screens and Theatres by State and Exhibitor, 2001–2011', January 2013, http://www.screenaustralia.gov.au/research/statistics/wcststateexhibit.asp (accessed 27 May 2013).

10. Karina Aveyard, 'Australian Films at the Cinema: Rethinking the Role of Distribution and Exhibition', *Media International Australia*, 138 (2011), 36-45 (p.40).

11. 'State of Cinema', address to the 56th San Francisco International Film Festival, April 2013, http://www.deadline.com/2013/04/steven-soderbergh-state-of-cinema-address/ (accessed 27 July 2013).

12. Screen Australia, 'Beyond the Box Office: Understanding Audiences in a Multi-Screen World', April 2011, p.17, http://www.screenaustralia.gov.au/getmedia/511b73c6-5276-4701-828c-46916e74f29d/Rpt_BeyondBoxOffice.pdf (accessed 20 August 2013).

13. Screen Australia, 'Beyond the Box Office', p.18 (accessed 20 August 2013).

14. Kathleen Drumm, 'Beyond the Cinema: Screen Australia Responds to Critique', 28 June 2013, http://screenhub.com.au/news/shownewsarticle.php?newsID=48622 (accessed 19 August 2013).

15. Don Groves, 'Solution Proposed for Offset Issue', 22 August 2013, http://if.com.au/2013/08/22/article/Solution-proposed-for-offset-issue/TLODOLTUGB.html (accessed 23 August 2013).

16. Alan Parker, 'Building a Sustainable UK Film Industry: A Presentation to the UK Film Industry', 5 November 2002,

British Film Industry, http://industry.bfi.org.uk/media/pdf/q/r/BaSFI.pdf (accessed 27 May 2013).

17. Quoted in Kirstin Murray, 'Australia Falls Short of Box-Office Expectations', *7.30 Report*, ABC TV, 1 December 2008, http://www.abc.net.au/7.30/content/2008/s2434699.htm (accessed 27 May 2013).

18. Maria De Rosa/Communications MDR, 'The Canadian Feature-Film Distribution Sector', in *Review: Trends, Policies and Market Developments*, research report, September 2012, p.74, http://www.omdc.on.ca/Assets/Research/Research+Reports/The+Canadian+Feature+Film+Distribution+Sector/The+Canadian+Feature+Film+Distribution+Sector+in+Review+Trends$!2c+Policies+and+Market+Developments.pdf (accessed 19 August 2013).

19. 'Save Your Legs!', *Sunday Age*, 24 February 2013, http://www.theage.com.au/entertainment/movies/save-your-legs-20130223-2exvf.html#ixzz2cOHz14KK (accessed 19 August 2013).

20. 'Grace Notes', *Sydney Morning Herald*, 30 April 2011, http://www.smh.com.au/entertainment/movies/grace-notes-20110428-1dxa9.html (accessed 19 August 2013).

21. Screen Australia, 'Research: Did You Know?', January 2012, http://www.screenaustralia.gov.au/news_and_events/bulletins/didyouknow/documents/DidUKnow_Jan12.pdf (accessed 27 May 2013).

22. Interview with the author, Sydney, 28 March 2012.

23. Brendan Swift, 'The Maltese Falcon', *Inside Film*, 144 (December-January 2012), p.26.

24. Sophie Raymond, Australian International Documentary Conference workshop, Adelaide, 28 February 2012.

25. Australian International Documentary Conference workshop, Adelaide, 28 February 2012.

26. mUmBRELLA, 'I Haven't Seen a Cent Out of *Bran Nue Dae*: Perkins', 3 May 2011, http://mumbrella.com.

au/i-havent-seen-a-cent-out-of-bran-nue-dae-perkins-8040 (accessed 27 May 2013).

27. Silver & Alpert, 'Digital Dawn', p.11.

28. Enzo Tedeschi, 'The Tunnel Infographic—One Year On', *The Tunnel* Blog, 25 June 2012, http://blog.thetunnel-movie.net/?p=868 (accessed 27 May 2013).

29. Harris, p.7.

30. Helen Klaebe & Rebecca Laycock, 'How to Work the Crowd: A Snapshot of Barriers and Motivations to Crowdfunding', report to Artsupport & Australia Council for the Arts, July 2012, pp.5-7, http://www.australiacouncil.gov.au/__data/assets/pdf_file/0017/132362/How_to_work_the_crowd_FINAL_300712.pdf (accessed 13 July 2013).

31. Elizabeth Gerber, Julie S. Hui & Pei-Yi Kuo, 'Crowdfunding: Why People are Motivated to Post and Fund Projects on Crowd-funding Platforms', *International Workshop on Design, Influence, and Social Technologies: Techniques, Impacts and Ethics, 2012 ACM Conference on Computer Supported Cooperative Work* (11-15 February 2012: Seattle, USA), http://distworkshop.files.wordpress.com/2012/01/dist2012_submission_11.pdf (accessed 20 August 2013).

32. Paul Chai, 'Oz Thriller "The Tunnel" Profits from Giving Film Away', *Variety*, 3 July 2012, http://variety.com/2012/film/news/oz-thriller-the-tunnel-profits-from-giving-film-away-1118056199/ (accessed 19 August 2013).

33. Studies by Jupiter Research in 2002, by music research firm The Leading Question in 2005 and a report by the BI Norwegian School of Management in 2009 offer three examples of how media pirates are also the most generous buyers, showing a strong correlation between downloading and paid consumption, and suggesting that shared files are not foregone sales, but a form of marketing.

34. Michael Bodey, 'New Data Lifts the Lid on

Video-On-Demand', *Australian*, 16 March 2013, http://www.theaustralian.com.au/arts/new-data-lifts-the-lid-on-video-on-demand/story-e6frg8n6-1226598570418 (accessed 20 August 2013)

35. Harris, p.56.

36. Australian International Documentary Conference workshop, Adelaide, 28 February 2012.

37. Ibid.

38. Screen Australia, 'What to Watch', p.7 (accessed 26 August 2013).

39. Screen Australia, 'Audiovisual Markets—Cinema—Box Office—By Admissions and Gross', February 2013, http://screenaustralia.gov.au/research/statistics/wcboadmission.asp (accessed 26 August 2013).

40. Screen Australia, 'What to Watch', p.2 (accessed 26 August 2013).

41. Ben Eltham, 'Australia Doesn't Need Better Films, Just Better Distribution', *Crikey.com*, 27 January 2012, http://www.crikey.com.au/2012/01/27/australia-doesnt-need-better-films-just-better-distribution/ (accessed 12 February 2012).

Readers' Forum

Responses to David Pledger's *Re-valuing the Artist in the New World Order*

PAT HOFFIE is a visual artist. She is Professor at Queensland College of Art, Griffith University.

Every once in a while there's a position paper that emerges like a comet of phosphorescent light to trace a burning trail across the vast velvety blackness of cultural policy skies. They're rare enough— perhaps one or two in a lifetime if you're lucky. And when a really good one bursts into ken, its mercurial orbit sheds light on new possibilities of how we in the arts interpret what we do. Or, alternately, they can remind you of why you fell in love with that night sky in the first place.

I can remember the first time a cultural discussion paper had that effect on me and those around me—the first was when David Throsby and Devon Mills' *When are you going to get a real job?: an economic study of Australian artists* emerged as a research report for the Australia Council in 1989. The second time happened recently when I read David Pledger's Platform Paper, *Re-valuing the Artist in the New World Order*.

On the first occasion it seemed as though, for the first time, the Australian arts sector had a way of arguing its worth—and its pitfalls—in demonstrable economic terms. Just as importantly, this paper served as an indicator that the sector could be collectively defined in a cohesive way. 'Back in the day', as it was, when the Australia Council for the Arts used to pride itself on being a think-tank—one that commissioned such reports and one that was deeply committed to 'grass-roots representation' in terms of the number of artists serving on its committees and boards.

Even further 'back in the day', artists had lobbied hard to develop an arts infrastructure that could function as a network to sustain their practice. The Australia Council was NOT the architecture of the cultural sector's infrastructure. It's all too easy to forget that artists were the architects of so much of the Australian arts infrastructure; that artists worked at grass-roots levels to build, develop and, ultimately, work towards a more 'professionalised' arts infrastructure when ongoing local, state and federal support was needed to keep the organisations running from year to year.

It's very important to remember this important aspect of history when you read David Pledger's *Re-valuing the Artist in the New World Order*, or you might end up making the mistake of thinking that somehow these 'faceless' organisations were just self-perpetuating from the start. Wrong. Pledger knows this, and he doesn't let artists today off the hook; he places full responsibility on the failure of those artists who have 'allow(ed) ourselves to be displaced from leadership, advisory and advocacy roles.' Looking back, romantics could be forgiven for thinking that with the success of building an arts sector has come the creation of its own kind of monster.

Victor Frankenstein had been wrong too. But he'd also dreamed his dream of creation fuelled by idealism and vision. It may well be that the monster of managerialism has not been dreamed up by the Australian arts sector on its own, but its particular monster is its own incarnation, and Pledger makes a plea that we the artists confront the current problems face-on. Pledger is succinct, convincing and inspiring in many of his claims, and for the sake of brevity I name three important ones:

(1) The arts sector has never been an 'arts industry' or a 'cultural industry' or an industry of any kind at all, and anyone who is still faffing round thinking they're part of it should wake up to the stark economic reality. There's a good chance that those who *do* believe this are part of the problem; read on:

(2) The monster of managerialism has turned on artists so that they too have made the mistake of dreaming themselves into being little dependent ersatz managers. As Pledger points out, 'artists spend disproportionately more time writing applications for funding their work than they do on making it'.

(3) Risk-taking is a lower-heart-beat necessity to art-making; but risk-taking has begun to seem like a rare exotic urge in the climate in which we're currently immersed. However Pledger wastes little time bemoaning the lack of understanding of the culture's value for contemporary Australia; rather, he defines issues, identifies targets, recognises problems and offers solutions. And he is collegial and inclusive in doing so. He describes the important role that the National Association of the Visual Arts (NAVA) has played as an effective lobbying and representational body to government. He alludes to the way Carrillo Gantner and Alison Carroll in their recent Platform Paper have defined the crucial importance that culture *must* play if Australia's role in 'the Asian Century' is to be played out most effectively. He celebrates the bravado and entrepreneurial spirit of David Walsh's MONA as an example of the best of what's possible here. And he critically responds to the importance of the issues raised in the National Cultural Policy.

Pledger's paper also has plenty of examples from other countries where the value of the arts are argued on the basis of 'public good' rather than as producers of commodities and cultural consumption. And he has examples of how Australia's myopically cheap focus on the managerial indicators of 'efficiency' and 'productivity' has not served the country well.

Critical thinking lies at the core of creative practice and, while it's a great practice for encouraging ingenuity, it can sometimes make the practitioner feel they're afloat on a rocky raft of possibilities. Artists inevitably sway between swagger and self-doubt, yet Pledger's paper leaves artists in no doubt that their practice *matters*. He reminds them, then he calls on them to act on this recognition collectively, cohesively and convincingly.

For too long now 'Professional Practices' courses in tertiary institutions have been taught as a kind of Mendicant's Manual for Fund-Seeking; where students are taught to be obedient form-fillers with little or no knowledge of the history that created their own little piece of managerial nightmare. Pledger's paper should be included as a must-read for all students at tertiary institutions, a kind of starter provocation that lets students know that things don't happen by chance, that structures can and should be challenged and, most importantly of all, that the chosen path they are paying so highly for *does* matter.

In Mary Shelley's 1818 novel the creator of the monster flees from the horror of his creation, refusing to confront the problems of his own making. Pledger makes a call for artists to face the demons they're partly responsible for creating and, in so doing, to imagine a 'new order' in Australian culture—one that starts by demanding a recognition of the primacy and value of, and a respect for, the role of the artist.

NICOLE BEYER is Director of Theatre Network Victoria, an advocate for the professional theatre industry, that works to strengthen independent and small to medium sectors and increase connection between all parts of the industry.

In *Revaluing the Artist in the New World Order*, David Pledger laments the time, more than ten years ago, when theatre artists in Victoria stopped asking for more funding to make work because they felt it was counter-productive.

David believes that 'artists are fearful of speaking up for fear of retribution in the form of unsuccessful grant applications or upsetting the gatekeepers, whose support is essential to getting up projects.'

I have seen this illustrated recently, again here in Victoria, when a new grants program, VicArts, was announced to replace the former suite of programs. This was without sector consultation and with eligibility changes that seriously affect the viability of some companies and the careers of some artists.

While some aims of the new program are, on the face of it, admirable, i.e. to streamline the application and assessment processes, and to remove some of the artificial, restrictive categories, the problems are significant. They include the short-sighted restriction that you can only have one active grant at a time, that is, you cannot even apply for another grant until your previous project is acquitted. This new restriction undermines and denies artists' processes, which are long-term and based on overlapping projects.

Economic imperatives clearly drive these changes— that limited government spending can be spread more thinly, with more artists making do with less support. This exemplifies David's key point that there's a shift from valuing social, cultural, environmental, and financial impacts to valuing only the latter. Economic efficiency is now seen as indisputably, almost innately, government's key goal.

It's a naive view that the work of artists are a series of independent projects that can be funded one at a time, or sporadically. What independent artists require is flexibility and an investment from funding bodies that acknowledges and supports their non-linear practice. As one of Theatre Network Victoria's members, an independent producer (wanting to remain anonymous), explained, 'established artists and producers are always working at development, presentation and touring stages of different works at any given time. It feels like this has not been understood in the new program.'

Significantly, the sector's response to the funding program changes has been exactly as David predicts— artists and companies are too afraid of repercussions should they speak up. Writing for ArtsHub on changes needed at Arts Victoria, Brian Benjamin says, 'Even those organisations that receive a few thousand dollars when tens of thousands are needed, dare not be critical of the hand that feeds them. Those who receive nothing live in hope that they might receive some next time.' (3 September 2013)

Theatre Network Victoria's members have contacted us to make clear their concerns, but most of them, including big, established companies, are unwilling to go directly to Arts Victoria to make a complaint. As David Pledger writes, they fear that they will be 'categorised as difficult, opinionated, outspoken'—in other words, trouble-makers who have everything to lose and nothing to gain from speaking out.

I believe that artists do care about making change; it isn't a lack of will that is the problem. One of the emerging themes of this year's Australian Theatre Forum was 'agency'. It was curator Alicia Talbot's guiding philosophy and it relates to this dilemma—how can we empower ourselves as artists to speak out confidently to make the change that is needed? It was also raised in the keynote by futurist Kristin Alford and anthropologist Lenore Manderson. They both spoke about the need to take action, and to become empowered again as a society. Lenore regretted the limited activism of today, compared to the self-determination of the late 1960s and 70s—when all of us, including artists, were out on the streets demanding change.

These conversations resonated throughout the forum with delegates hungry for provocation and inspiration so that they could rediscover their own agency and power—to renew their confidence to step up and speak out against the sorts of challenges that David articulates. Indeed, his final chapter is a 'necessary series of provocations'. His provocation titled Agency is for funding bodies to fund artists directly to increase their autonomy and allow them to determine how to present their work. He proposes that funding should be shifted from infrastructure projects to fellowships directly for artists—again to put the artist at the centre of the arts.

The Sidney Myer Foundation's creative fellowship program works in this way, acknowledging that the artist is the best person to decide how to spend their grant, and that artists 'need time to develop and practise their vocation in circumstances which support reflection and encourage risk taking'. Funding bodies need to take a more respectful and trusting approach to funding artists, and value the long-term processes and intersecting nature of different phases of work. I support David's proposition that funding should be put back into the hands of artists, rather than going to producers or presenters or other infrastructure.

But the funding bodies won't change if they aren't hearing that they need to.

'We have to put our hand up', David says, 'Speak up. Refuse to back down for fear of retribution. Ask for more. When we don't get it, demand it…Advocate for the arts as a public good…Arm ourselves with facts, figures, passion and rigour….Do not remain silent.'

I endorse these provocations and I thank David for his honest, smart and hopeful paper.

FORTHCOMING

PP38 February 2014
ENLIGHTENMENT OR ENTITLEMENT?
Rethinking tertiary music education

Tertiary music education is commonly understood as preparing students for a career as a performer. This, however, fails to address fundamental shifts in the ways most of us now typically encounter, and think about, music in our lives; nor does it acknowledge the diminishing funding base that supports traditional modes of teaching. It is time to rethink both how, and why, we teach music on campus.

In addressing the issues the author draws upon his experience since being appointed in 2012 to lead the government-initiated takeover by Australian National University of the revered Canberra School of Music, a time of intense controversy. His central premise is that the problem is at root *not financial, or organisational, but ethical.* Music institutions have, it seems, lost sight of, and failed to invigorate, the social contract that lies behind any public commitment to fund arts education. Tregear examines the changing culture and shows how his solutions are being applied in Canberra.

PETER TREGEAR is a prize-winning performer, author and music academic. A doctoral graduate of King's College Cambridge, he has held teaching positions in both the UK and Australia. In July 2012 he was appointed Head of School and Professor of Music at the School of Music of the Australian National University.

AT YOUR LOCAL BOOKSHOP FROM 1 FEBRUARY
AND AS A PAPERBACK OR ON LINE
FROM OUR WEBSITE AT
WWW.CURRENCYHOUSE.ORG.AU

Copyright Information